¡Tropicalismo!

¡Tropicalismo!

Spice Up Your Garden with Cannas, Bananas, and 93 Other Eye-Catching Tropical Plants

PAM BAGGETT

TIMBER PRESS
PORTLAND · LONDON

Text and photographs by Pam Baggett.
Copyright © 2008 by Pam Baggett. All rights reserved.

Published in 2008 by Timber Press, Inc.

The Haseltine Building
133 S.W. Second Avenue, Suite 450
Portland, Oregon 97204-3527
www.timberpress.com

2 The Quadrant
135 Salusbury Road
United Kingdom
www.timberpress.co.uk

Printed in China

Library of Congress Cataloging-in-Publication Data
Baggett, Pam.
  Tropicalismo!: spice up your garden with cannas, bananas, and 93 other
eye-catching tropical plants / Pam Baggett.
      p. cm.
  ISBN-13: 978-0-88192-947-8 (alk. paper)
  1. Tropical plants. 2. Gardening. I. Title.
  QK936.B34 2008
  635.9'523—dc22
                                                              2008008876

A catalog record for this book is also available from the British Library

KEY TO PLANT CARE SYMBOLS

LIGHT REQUIREMENTS

 SUN
Plant receives six hours or more
of direct sun every day

 PART SUN
Plant receives three to six hours
of direct sun every day

 LIGHT SHADE
Plant receives less than three hours
of direct sun and gets dappled sun
at other times during the day

 SHADE
Plant receives little or no direct sun,
only dappled sun

MOISTURE REQUIREMENTS

 HEAVY
Plant needs constantly moist soil

 MODERATE
Plant needs moderate moisture—
the surface of the soil can dry out
between waterings

 LIGHT
Plant tolerates some dryness—
the top inch or two of the soil
can dry out between waterings

INTRODUCTION

CRAZY FOR COLOR? Gone bonkers over big leaves? Tropical plants couldn't be easier to grow, and average-to-rich soil and a moderate amount of water produce spectacular results. Set out after spring nights remain above fifty degrees, bananas rocket up to ten feet, elephant ears send forth gigantic three-foot leaves, and flowering plants like lantana and cuphea produce hundreds of radiant blooms. Don't be misled by hardiness zones, which indicate only where a plant will overwinter. Tropicals thrive as warm-season annuals throughout most of the United States. So go ahead—energize your garden with the glittering hues and over-the-top textures of fast-growing tropical plants.

Abutilon megapotamicum 'Little Imp'

TRAILING ABUTILON

PRONOUNCED
uh-BEW-tih-lon
meg-uh-poe-TAM-ih-kum

CARE NEEDS

THE DELICATE BLOSSOMS of *Abutilon* 'Little Imp' dangle like small lanterns from dark three-foot stems, their shy lemon petals peering from beneath showy red calyces. 'Little Imp' holds its branches outward rather than up, so that they insinuate themselves among nearby plants. Treated as an annual, it flowers from early summer until hard frost; where it's hardy, 'Little Imp' grows five feet tall and blooms almost year-round. It's a tough plant that remains green until several hard freezes send it into dormancy. Its flowers look sweet mingled with *Plectranthus* 'Green on Green', *Solenostemon* 'New Hurricane', and *Pennisetum setaceum* 'Rubrum'. Overwinters in zones 7–10.

Acalypha pendula
STRAWBERRY FIRETAIL
CHENILLE PLANT

ALSO SOLD AS
Acalypha repens

PRONOUNCED
**ack-uh-LIFE-uh
PEN-dew-luh**

**ack-uh-LIFE-uh
REE-penz**

CARE NEEDS

STRAWBERRY FIRETAIL'S CARPET of fuzzy green leaves seems to be crawling with three-inch-long, fruity-red caterpillars. But those colorful critters are actually woolly flowering catkins that appear all season long. Snip the spent blossoms once they turn brown, and give strawberry firetail average-to-rich, evenly moist soil, where it will make a two-foot-wide seasonal groundcover. Strawberry firetail also excels as a trailing plant for containers. Create a red-and-gold combination with *Canna* 'Australia', *Duranta* 'Aurea', and *Sanchezia speciosa*; or celebrate July all summer with *Salvia* 'Indigo Spires' and white-flowered *Hedychium coronarium*. Overwinters in zones 7b–10.

Acalypha wilkesiana 'Cypress Elf'

COPPERLEAF

PRONOUNCED
**ack-uh-LIFE-uh
wilks-ee-AY-nuh**

CARE NEEDS

ACALYPHA 'CYPRESS ELF' looks like one of those cartoon characters that sticks its fork in an electric socket and explodes! Its ruddy chocolate leaves edged in coral-pink are five inches long and only a half-inch wide—they're crowded onto upright two-foot stems where they dangle like tentacles that wave in a breeze. Let's face it: 'Cypress Elf' is as strange as some oddball undersea creature, but it's a cool kind of weird. Like other acalyphas, 'Cypress Elf' tolerates extreme heat but not drought; ensure ample water to prevent leaf drop. It's delightful with *Abutilon* 'Little Imp', *Phormium* 'Atropurpureum', and big brother *Acalypha* 'Obovata'. Overwinters in zones 9–10.

Acalypha wilkesiana 'Macafeeana'

COPPERLEAF

PRONOUNCED
ack-uh-LIFE-uh
wilks-ee-AY-nuh

CARE NEEDS

DEPENDING ON SOIL fertility and light levels, a single eight-inch leaf of this resplendent acalypha may sport splashes of copper and crimson, sunset pink and chocolate. Strong sun and average-to-rich soil produce hot, saturated colors, while in shadier sites the pigments pale to soft, simmering pastels. A soil in declining fertility (a container in late season, for instance) yields mostly red and bronze foliage. In any location, three-foot-tall *Acalypha* 'Macafeeana' offers daring design opportunities for gardeners willing to venture beyond the comfort of traditional colors. Leap into new territory and combine 'Macafeeana' with *Fuchsia* 'Gartenmeister Bonstedt', *Saccharum* 'Pele's Smoke', and calico plant, *Alternanthera ficoidea*. Overwinters in zones 9–10.

Acalypha wilkesiana 'Obovata'

CHOCOLATE COPPERLEAF

PRONOUNCED
ack-uh-LIFE-uh
wilks-ee-AY-nuh

CARE NEEDS

PICTURE DOWNWARD-DANGLING milk chocolate leaves, their edges trimmed in the radiant coral tones of a tropical reef. Or if that doesn't work for you, imagine painting the rims of your beagle dog's ears—either way, you get an image of five-foot-tall *Acalypha* 'Obovata'. Its burnished, six-inch leaves make a foliar show that lasts until frost, which more than makes up for its inconspicuous flowering catkins. For a dreamy effect, try 'Obovata' with *Lantana* 'Pink Caprice' and cream-and-pink *Solenostemon* 'Aurora'. Or create the visual equivalent of Vesuvius erupting by combining 'Obovata' with *Salvia* 'Caribbean Coral' and fire-striped *Canna* 'Phaison'. Overwinters in zones 9–10.

Allamanda 'Cherries Jubilee'

PRONOUNCED
al-uh-MAN-duh

CARE NEEDS

FROM SUMMER TO frost, *Allamanda* 'Cherries Jubilee' opens five-inch blossoms whose exquisite color will make you crave black-cherry ice cream. The color intensifies in the flower's throat, and it deepens throughout the petals in cooler weather. Three-inch, vibrant green leaves on scrambling stems make a good backdrop for the exotic blossoms. Five-foot-tall 'Cherries Jubilee' is a vining plant, but it lacks hooks or tendrils, so plan to train it up its support. Grown in containers, some stems drape over the edges while most weave through other plants. Easy-to-grow 'Cherries Jubilee' prefers average-to-moist soil, where it thrives with *Colocasia* 'Black Magic' and *Centaurea* 'Colchester White'. Overwinters in zones 9–10.

Alocasia 'Hilo Beauty'
SPOTTED ELEPHANT EAR

PRONOUNCED
al-uh-KAY-zhah

CARE NEEDS

COMPARED TO ITS monumental brethren, *Alocasia* 'Hilo Beauty' is a small plant that grows only two feet tall. Its twelve-inch leaves are spectacularly marked with creamy spots that give them endearing personalities, like the eager faces of a litter of puppies. Looking beyond its obvious attractiveness, 'Hilo Beauty' serves an important garden function: it brings bold texture down to the lower reaches of the border, where leaves tend to be small and in need of contrast. Like other elephant ears, 'Hilo Beauty' can be grown in water gardens, or plant it in average-to-moist soil with *Cyperus papyrus*, *Hedychium* 'Flaming Torch', and calico plant, *Alternanthera ficoidea*. Overwinters in zones 9–10.

Alocasia 'Portodora'

UPRIGHT ELEPHANT EAR

PRONOUNCED
al-uh-KAY-zhuh

CARE NEEDS

ALOCASIA **'PORTODORA' IS** guaranteed to give your garden that Gilligan's Island look! Rocketing up to eight feet tall, its fat purplish stalks support enormous three-foot leaves. Rather than hanging downward like most elephant ears, 'Portodora' points its leaves straight up, like giant arrows aimed at the sky. Who could ask for a more emphatic, exclamatory focal point? A hybrid of *Alocasia odora* and *A. portei*, glossy green 'Portodora' holds its baby plantlets tucked tight against the mother bulb. It prefers moist soil and looks its tropical best with *Musa basjoo*, sleek green-and-yellow *Alpinia zerumbet* 'Variegata', and chartreuse *Ipomoea* 'Margarita'. Overwinters in zones 7b–10.

Alpinia zerumbet 'Variegata'

VARIEGATED SHELL GINGER

PRONOUNCED
**al-PIN-ee-uh
ZAIR-um-bet**

CARE NEEDS

THE TROPICAL GINGER clan is huge and includes this wonderful alpinia, grown for its foot-long, fresh-waxed leaves streaked with green and lemon-yellow. In size and shape, two-foot-tall *Alpinia* 'Variegata' looks like a tropical hosta, but it holds its color in heat rather than fading in intensity as hostas sometimes do. It works beautifully in borders, but 'Variegata' offers a form critical to well-designed containers: it holds many of its leaves horizontally, filling the outward space between a dominant upward plant and those necessary downward trailers. Colorfast in sun or shade, 'Variegata' looks handsome with *Alocasia* 'Portodora' and chartreuse sweet potato, *Ipomoea* 'Margarita'. Overwinters in zones 8–10.

Alternanthera dentata 'Rubiginosa'

BLOODLEAF CHRISTMAS CLOVER

PRONOUNCED
all-tur-NAN-thur-uh den-TAY-tuh

CARE NEEDS

THE SATURATED BURGUNDY foliage of *Alternanthera* 'Rubiginosa' brings out the best in both pastels and deeper shades. Its two-inch leaves are borne on thirty-inch burgundy stems that roam through their companions, uniting the composition. Unless you overwinter 'Rubiginosa', don't expect to see flowers—the common name Christmas clover refers to its papery off-white pompoms that appear in winter. Don't worry, 'Rubiginosa' is so pretty you won't miss them. Try it with hot orange *Hamelia patens*, chartreuse *Ipomoea* 'Margarita', and gold-striped *Canna* 'Bengal Tiger'; or achieve rubiginosal elegance with *Petunia integrifolia* and lacy *Centaurea* 'Colchester White'. Overwinters in zones 9–10.

Alternanthera ficoidea—calico form

CALICO PLANT
JOSEPH'S COAT
PARROT LEAF

PRONOUNCED
**all-tur-NAN-thur-uh
fie-KOY-dee-uh**

CARE NEEDS

YOU'D HARDLY THINK calico plant's small cupped leaves could contain so many colors, yet on a single twelve-inch-tall plant you'll find pinks ranging from soft to shocking, pale orange, creamy gold, grass green, and yummy chocolate patches where the pink and green mix. Intense sun deepens the colors, while in part shade they pale to delicate pastel shades. Tiny cloverlike blooms occasionally appear in the leaf axils but hold no interest compared to the tropical fruit-salad foliage. Calico plant grows eighteen inches wide and makes an exotic carpet for *Acalypha* 'Obovata', *Canna* 'Phaison', and *Xanthosoma* 'Lime Zinger'. Overwinters in zones 9–10.

Alternanthera ficoidea 'Red Threads'

PRONOUNCED
all-tur-NAN-thur-uh
fie-KOY-dee-uh

CARE NEEDS

SIX-INCH-TALL *ALTERNANTHERA* 'RED THREADS' creates a jeweled ruby carpet at your feet—what a welcome sight after a long day at work! Its fine-textured foliage only looks delicate, though—'Red Threads' is a vigorous grower that tolerates drought and heat. A single plant spreads thirty inches wide, but you'll need more than one, for 'Red Threads' can be used in so many ways: entwined with *Oxalis spiralis* 'Aureus' in a Victorian knot pattern; spilling from containers filled with wine-red *Salvia* 'Van Houttei' and blazing *Solenostemon* 'New Hurricane'; or fronting a border planted with *Canna* 'Australia', gold-striped *Sanchezia speciosa*, and chartreuse *Duranta* 'Aurea'. Overwinters in zones 9–10.

Ananas comosus 'Variegatus'
VARIEGATED PINEAPPLE

PRONOUNCED
AN-uh-nus ko-MO-sus

CARE NEEDS

IT'S A PARADOX: striped with bands of white, pink, and green, the three-foot leaves of *Ananas* 'Variegatus' couldn't be prettier, but be careful—they're armed with toothed, flesh-piercing barbs that line the leaf edges. One of the loveliest tender plants available to temperate zone gardeners, 'Variegatus' is a multicolored selection of the edible pineapple plant. It grows slowly to four feet tall and is well worth overwintering, for older plants may produce small sweet fruits topped with striped foliage. Give 'Variegatus' a site with excellent drainage and provide the reliable moisture pineapples prefer. *Pentas* 'Dorann's Pink' and *Talipariti* 'Tricolor' make lively companions. Overwinters in zone 10.

Begonia carolinifolia

PALM-LEAF BEGONIA

PRONOUNCED
**bih-GO-nyuh
kar-oh-lie-nih-FO-lee-uh**

CARE NEEDS

PALM-LEAF BEGONIA IS a wondrous plant, with huge palmate leaves made up of several ten-inch, arching leaflets. The glossy, forest-green leaves have deep red undersides, and they spring from fleshy tubers on two-foot burgundy petioles. An entire leaf reaches almost two feet across, making a spectacular contrast to fine-textured plants. In spring, palm-leaf begonia produces stick-straight stems that bear creamy white blossoms—the flowers aren't nearly as showy, though, as its captivating foliage. Palm-leaf begonia thrives in heat; in most hardiness zones, it tolerates morning sun. Create a rubied textural tapestry by combining it with *Solenostemon* 'Religious Radish' and creeping jewelweed, *Impatiens repens*. Overwinters in zones 9–10.

Breynia disticha 'Roseo-picta'

PINK SNOWBUSH

PRONOUNCED
BRAY-nee-uh die-STICK-uh

CARE NEEDS

TONE DOWN SUMMER'S sizzling heat with the cool, refreshing foliage of *Breynia* 'Roseo-picta'. Each inch-long oval leaflet is a marbled confection of sunset pink, milky white, and soft green (though in older leaves green and white predominate). The red-tinged branches have an intriguing texture—they zigzag from one node to the next, while the pinnate leaves arch elegantly from each node. Where it's hardy, 'Roseo-picta' grows to be a five-foot shrub; used as an annual, it makes a thirty-inch-tall centerpiece for containers or well-drained borders. Contrast its delicate texture with bold-leaved *Colocasia* 'Black Magic' and *Solenostemon* 'Mariposa'. Overwinters in zones 9–10.

Brugmansia 'Sunset'

VARIEGATED ANGEL'S TRUMPET

PRONOUNCED
brug-MAN-see-uh

CARE NEEDS

BRUGMANSIAS ARE THE queen of flowering tropicals, their huge trumpet-shaped blossoms belting out a powerful, powder-sweet fragrance that perfumes the night air. In addition to its smooth-as-silk, soft peach trumpets, *Brugmansia* 'Sunset' sports foot-long leaves painted a subtle blend of celadon, sage, and creamy white. The nine-inch-long blossoms dangle like bells from the leaf axils and are borne in flushes of fifty or more blooms on a mature plant. Treated as an annual, 'Sunset' grows three to four feet tall; where it's hardy, it reaches six to eight feet. *Solenostemon* 'Aurora' and peach-flowered *Cuphea ignea* provide pleasing color echoes. Overwinters in zones 7b–10.

Canna 'Australia'

ALSO SOLD AS
Canna 'Feuerzauber'

PRONOUNCED
KAN-uh

CARE NEEDS

CANNA 'AUSTRALIA' COMMANDS attention with the deepest burgundy-black foliage ever seen in the world of cannas. Unlike other dark-leaved selections, its glossy eighteen-inch leaves hold their saturated color without fading in summer heat, especially if you provide the rich, moist soil cannas prefer. As if fantastic foliage wasn't enough, 'Australia' knocks you backward with high-wattage, heartthrob-red flowers that top the five-foot stalks from summer to frost. 'Australia' makes a powerful backdrop for white-variegated *Plectranthus coleoides* and *Breynia* 'Roseo-picta'. Or combine it with red-and-yellow *Abutilon* 'Little Imp', *Salvia elegans*, *Solenostemon* 'New Hurricane', and chartreuse sweet potato, *Ipomoea* 'Margarita'. Overwinters in zones 7b–10.

Canna 'Bengal Tiger'

ALSO SOLD AS
C. generalis
'Aureostriata',
C. 'Pretoria'

PRONOUNCED
KAN-uh

CARE NEEDS

ZAP YOUR GARDEN with color, energy, and excitement—plant *Canna* 'Bengal Tiger'! Its striped green-and-gold leaves make an electrifying focal point, while its brilliant tangerine blooms on smoky pink stems stand out like torches against the sky. Six-foot-tall 'Bengal Tiger' flowers from summer to frost—provide rich, moist soil or grow it in your water garden. Scared to plant something so gaudy? Risk it—after all, life is meant to be reveled in. Once you see the change 'Bengal Tiger' brings to your garden, you'll never look back. *Colocasia* 'Black Magic', *Lantana* 'Desert Sunset', and *Cuphea cyanea* make exquisite companions. Overwinters in zones 7–10.

Canna 'Constitution'

PRONOUNCED
KAN-uh

CARE NEEDS

WHILE MANY CANNAS are shamelessly ostentatious, five-foot-tall *Canna* 'Constitution' offers subtle, sophisticated color that enhances pastel displays but also works with stronger shades. Its creamy chocolate-purple foliage provides a beautiful complement to the delicate shell pink flowers that appear from summer to frost. 'Constitution' prefers rich, well-watered soil but accepts average soil and moisture, particularly if you provide a good mulch. Where they aren't hardy, the tubers of 'Constitution' and other cannas can be dug in fall and overwintered in a cool but frost-free location. Create a satisfying quartet with 'Constitution', creamy pink *Solenostemon* 'Aurora', lacy *Lantana* 'Mozelle', and chocolate sugarcane, *Saccharum* 'Pele's Smoke'. Overwinters in zones 7–10.

Canna iridiflora 'Ehemanni'

PRONOUNCED
**KAN-uh
ih-rid-ih-FLORE-uh**

CARE NEEDS

OVERSIZED EIGHT-FOOT STEMS carry the graceful blooms of *Canna* 'Ehemanni' aloft, where they hang in elegant pendulous clusters. The warm cerise-pink petal color combined with the flower's weeping form gives 'Ehemanni' a different personality than most other cannas, whose blobby blossoms can seem brash by comparison. 'Ehemanni' is no lightweight, though. It's a vigorous grower, especially in rich, well-watered soil. Allow lots of elbow room, and plan on its huge, two- to three-foot leaves attracting attention as a prominent focal point for the back of the border. Chocolate-colored *Saccharum* 'Pele's Smoke', *Talipariti tiliaceum* 'Tricolor', and pink-and-white variegated pineapple (*Ananas* 'Variegatus') make beautiful companions. Overwinters in zones 7–10.

Canna 'Phaison'

ALSO SOLD AS
Canna **Tropicanna**

PRONOUNCED
KAN-uh

CARE NEEDS

UNPACK YOUR MAGIC markers and paint yourself a canna! To create *Canna* 'Phaison' (also known as Tropicanna), draw stripes of coral-red, yellow, burgundy, and black-green to cover the surface of its giant eighteen-inch leaves. Top the seven-foot stems with flaming tangerine flowers that appear from early summer to frost. Place your plants where the sun can backlight the leaves, setting them aflame. Give 'Phaison' your richest soil, fire-hose it regularly, and it will burn with intensity all season. You'll need strong companions to stand up to its heat—add to the conflagration with *Salvia* 'Caribbean Coral', *Pennisetum* 'Rubrum', *Xanthosoma* 'Lime Zinger', *Ensete* 'Maurelii', and chartreuse *Ipomoea* 'Margarita'. Overwinters in zones 7b–10.

Capsicum annuum— variegated form

VARIEGATED HOT PEPPER

PRONOUNCED
KAP-sih-kum AN-you-um

CARE NEEDS

VARIEGATED HOT PEPPER is a spicy little annual that deserves a place in your ornamental plantings, where it can parade its inch-long, inky-purple leaves flecked with white and green. Its tiny white flowers are typical of pepper plants, but the fruits that follow emerge pitch-black and ripen to fiery red. Variegated hot pepper is easy from seed; plants grow about thirty inches tall. Select the best-variegated seedlings, and give them the same conditions you would pepper plants in the vegetable garden: sunshine, rich soil, and plentiful water. Variegated hot pepper makes a festive underplanting for *Tibouchina urvilleana* and *Xanthosoma* 'Albomarginatum'. Overwinters in zones 9–10.

Centaurea gymnocarpa 'Colchester White'

VELVET CENTAUREA

SILVER BACHELOR'S BUTTONS

PRONOUNCED
**sen-tore-EE-uh
jim-no-KAR-puh**

CARE NEEDS

A SHIMMERING SILVER-LEAVED beauty, Centaurea 'Colchester White' produces glow-in-the-dark mounds of delicate, lacy foliage that forms a thirty-inch-wide, two-foot-tall mound. It's far more vigorous and attractive than the commonly grown silver annual known as dusty miller (Senecio cineraria), and while 'Colchester White' resembles a hardy artemesia, it's not invasive like artemesias often are. In late spring, 'Colchester White' produces pale purple bachelor-button flowers on thirty-inch stems, although these are less exciting than its tremendously valuable foliage. (Cut the flowers for bouquets, so your plants will produce new growth.) 'Colchester White' appreciates well-drained soil; it's stunning with purple Strobilanthes dyerianus and Tibouchina urvilleana. Overwinters in zones 8–10.

Cissus discolor
REX BEGONIA VINE

PRONOUNCED
SIS-us DIS-kul-ur

CARE NEEDS

GARDENERS ARE A worshipful lot, and most breathe a deep sigh of astounded gratitude when they first see rex begonia vine. It's a gorgeous plant whose silver- and pink-painted green leaves ascend climbing stems to ten feet or taller. The burgundy stems attach themselves to trellises with curling tendrils that look strangely like those used by grapevines, and indeed, rex begonia vine is a member of the grape family. It loves rich moist soil but scorches in full sun, so provide morning sun or light shade. Rex begonia vine can scale trellises, trail from containers, or scramble among *Alocasia* 'Portodora', *Strobilanthes dyerianus*, and *Oplismenus* 'Variegatus'. Overwinters in zone 10.

Colocasia antiquorum 'Illustris'

TARO
ELEPHANT EAR

PRONOUNCED
**koll-uh-KAY-zhuh
an-tih-KWOR-um**

CARE NEEDS

HOW MANY TRULY black plants can you name? (No fair counting those killed by frost!) Charcoal-black *Colocasia* 'Illustris' makes a stellar focal point from the moment it unfurls its first leaf; veined with green, the eighteen-inch leaves look like x-rays of a Martian rib cage. Plant thirty-inch-tall 'Illustris' in moist soil or in your water garden, but never let it wilt: when elephant ears dehydrate, the leaves turn crispy brown. As it grows, 'Illustris' produces numerous new plantlets around the parent bulb. Create a sexy combo with *Centaurea* 'Colchester White', *Solenostemon* 'Fishnet Stockings', and rosy *Crinum* 'Ellen Bosanquet'. Overwinters in zones 7–10.

Colocasia esculenta 'Black Magic'

TARO
ELEPHANT EAR

PRONOUNCED
**koll-uh-KAY-zhuh
es-kew-LEN-tuh**

CARE NEEDS

THE CARDS ARE turned, their secrets read: no one escapes the spell of *Colocasia* 'Black Magic'! Your eyes lock onto its smoky black leaves, and you know you've been captured. 'Black Magic' makes an unforgettable focal point, its two-foot leaves borne on five-foot, black-cherry stems. Give it a moist, sunny site; in most climates, shade turns 'Black Magic' a disappointing greenish purple. Its dusky leaves make a compelling backdrop for almost any other color—plant a coals-and-flames combination with orange *Cuphea* 'David Verity'; contrast its stark drama with *Centaurea* 'Colchester White'; or combine it with pink *Solenostemon* 'Mariposa' and *Breynia* 'Roseo-picta'. Overwinters in zones 7b–10.

Colocasia fallax
TARO
ELEPHANT EAR

PRONOUNCED
**koll-uh-KAY-zhuh
FAL-acks**

CARE NEEDS

IF YOU'VE ONLY grown gargantuan elephant ears with in-your-face impact, you might be surprised by fifteen-inch-tall *Colocasia fallax*. Elegant and compact, it produces four-inch-long, bluish green leaves that pale to shimmering silver along the leaf veins. The contrast of the matte green coloring and reflective silver markings gives an intriguing three-dimensional look to the foliage. *Colocasia fallax* makes lots of beautiful babies as it grows; given rich, moist soil, it will fill a three-gallon container or form a two-foot-wide seasonal groundcover. It makes a dynamic foliage trio with *Curcuma* 'Emperor' and dainty *Oxalis* 'Aureus'. Overwinters in zones 7b–10.

Crinum 'Ellen Bosanquet'

PRONOUNCED
KRY-num

CARE NEEDS

FROM EARLY SUMMER until frost, *Crinum* 'Ellen Bosanquet' bears two-foot spikes of trumpet-shaped, deep rose-pink flowers that perfume the garden with their spicy sweetness. Its bold rosettes of succulent, strappy foliage resemble that of its close cousin, the amaryllis. Though 'Ellen Bosanquet' blooms best with adequate moisture, it's tougher than its elegant beauty implies, tolerating drought, monsoon, wicked heat, coastal sand, and sticky clay. A vigorous grower, 'Ellen Bosanquet' produces a generous number of offsets. Crinums are famed in the southern United States as long-lived, hardy bulbs; elsewhere, 'Ellen Bosanquet' can be dug and overwintered. *Canna* 'Ehemanni', *Talipariti tiliaceum* 'Tricolor', and *Solenostemon* 'Mariposa' provide colorful companionship. Overwinters in zones 7–10.

Cuphea cyanea
BLACK-EYED CUPHEA

PRONOUNCED
KEW-fee-uh sy-AN-ee-uh

CARE NEEDS

CUPHEA CYANEA WILL capture your heart with its petite pink and yellow flowers. The colors are primary, like shades you pulled from your first crayon box, but that also makes them primal: basic to your understanding and use of color. Done right, pink and yellow create an exuberant combination reminiscent of sunsets and summertime carnivals. Dainty inch-long leaves contribute to the delicate appearance of eighteen-inch-tall *Cuphea cyanea*. Drought resistance and the ability to attract hummingbirds are other appealing features. Pink-and-gold *Lantana* 'Desert Sunset' makes an excellent partner; add sophistication to the combination with bronze *Phormium* 'Atropurpureum' and *Talipariti tiliaceum* 'Tricolor'. Overwinters in zones 7–10.

Cuphea 'David Verity'

PRONOUNCED
KEW-fee-uh

CARE NEEDS

THESE FIERY FLOWERS will have hummingbirds flocking to your garden! *Cuphea* 'David Verity' boasts orange-red tubular blossoms tipped in yellow, borne on thirty-inch stems. The flowers appear from spring to frost, and they're made more beautiful by contrast with the plant's plum-stained green leaves and ruby stems. 'David Verity' has a handsome vase shape; when grown in the tight quarters of a container, its branches maneuver through its container-mates and unify the planting. Drought-resistant 'David Verity' works well in the border, too, asking only for decent soil drainage and plenty of sun. *Canna* 'Phaison', *Colocasia* 'Black Magic', and *Hibiscus* 'Jungle Red' make excellent partners. Overwinters in zones 8–10.

Cuphea hyssopifolia—chartreuse leaf form

CHARTREUSE MEXICAN HEATHER

PRONOUNCED
KEW-fee-uh
hiss-op-ih-FO-lee-uh

CARE NEEDS

MANY GARDENERS KNOW what a floriferous plant Mexican heather is—it produces a non-stop profusion of tiny rosy purple flowers against a backdrop of petite green leaves. It's a sweet and serviceable plant, tough and drought tolerant, though hardly a stunner. But check out the chartreuse form of Mexican heather, which adds shiny yellow foliage against which the little purple flowers leap to prominence. Growing fourteen inches tall, it forms a tight bun of shocking color that resembles English heather (*Calluna vulgaris*) in texture, hence its common name. Chartreuse Mexican heather looks gorgeous in well-drained, sunny borders or containers with purple *Strobilanthes dyerianus*, *Stachytarpheta jamaicensis*, and *Senna didymotropa*. Overwinters in zones 8b–10.

Cuphea ignea— peach-flowered form

PEACH FIRECRACKER PLANT

PRONOUNCED
KEW-fee-uh IG-nee-uh

CARE NEEDS

MANY GARDENERS GROW the incendiary orange form of *Cuphea ignea* known as cigar plant, but few have seen its pastel peach sibling, which produces hundreds of inch-long blossoms over a season that stretches from…well, actually peach firecracker plant just never quits blooming. (It flowers all winter if you provide a sunny greenhouse.) Tiny green leaves with white midribs enhance the dainty blooms; so do all the hummingbirds lured by its blossoms. For all its winsome delicacy, sixteen-inch-tall peach firecracker plant is drought resistant and impervious to heat. Its makes a beautiful contrast to bold-textured tropicals, like cream-speckled *Alocasia* 'Hilo Beauty' and peach-flowered *Brugmansia* 'Sunset'. Overwinters in zones 8b–10.

Curcuma petiolata 'Emperor'

VARIEGATED HIDDEN CONE GINGER

PRONOUNCED
kur-KEW-muh
pet-ee-oh-LAY-tuh

CARE NEEDS

A BOLD TROPICAL for shady sites, *Curcuma* 'Emperor' bears eighteen-inch, pleated green leaves bordered by a wide band of refreshing white. Given decent soil and occasional watering, it looks handsome and happy even through the heat of summer, when lesser plants seem perpetually stressed. Two-foot-tall 'Emperor' produces curious but attractive flowers in early summer. Tucked against the base of the stems, the blooms resemble pine cones whose white or pale pink bracts enclose small golden flowers. Though elegant enough to solo in containers, 'Emperor' also sparkles with *Alocasia* 'Portodora', *Fuchsia* 'Gartenmeister Bonstedt', and white ginger lily, *Hedychium coronarium*. Overwinters in zones 7b–10.

Cyperus papyrus
EGYPTIAN PAPER PLANT
BULRUSH

PRONOUNCED
SY-pur-us puh-PY-rus

CARE NEEDS

THE NILE RIVER is home to *Cyperus papyrus*, the plant from which the Egyptians first made paper. Atop its leafless, triangular six-foot stems, silken green bracts burst into trailing green fireworks—or a mop of shaggy green hair, depending on your perspective. From June through September, little green seed spikelets form among the bracts and mature to russet brown. Egyptian paper plant prefers moist-to-soggy conditions and would love a spot in your water garden. Contrast its airy texture with brazen *Canna* 'Bengal Tiger' and *Colocasia* 'Black Magic', or create a green-and-black combo with *Colocasia* 'Illustris' and *Solenostemon* 'Fishnet Stockings'. Overwinters in zones 9–10.

Dianella 'Yellow Stripe'

FLAX LILY

PRONOUNCED
dye-uh-NEL-uh

CARE NEEDS

AS ITS NAME implies, *Dianella* 'Yellow Stripe' has striped green and yellow leaves—in texture it resembles a clump of variegated daylily foliage. Big deal, right? Actually it is, for this tough-as-nails tropical looks equally colorful in sun or shade, dry or moist soil. When its autumn flower spikes emerge, they offer a surprising twist: the wiry two-foot stems bear tiny lily-like blossoms that are an unlikely, stormy blue-gray. Use twenty-inch-tall 'Yellow Stripe' anywhere its reliable color and grassy texture are needed. It looks fabulous with feathery *Cyperus papyrus*, *Salvia* 'Van Houttei', *Alocasia* 'Portodora', and *Acalypha pendula*. Overwinters in zones 8–10.

Duranta erecta 'Aurea'

DWARF GOLDEN PIGEONBERRY

PRONOUNCED
dur-AN-tuh ih-RECK-tuh

CARE NEEDS

IF YOU'VE BEEN searching for a chartreuse foliage plant that takes hot summer sun without scorching or turning green, say hello to *Duranta* 'Aurea', a dwarf form of pigeonberry shrub that sports dainty two-inch, lemon-lime leaves. Drought tolerant and undemanding, 'Aurea' grows two feet tall and thirty inches wide. Though it sends forth an occasional spray of violet-blue blooms (which may be followed by deep golden berries), 'Aurea' is usually content to serve as a foliar beacon in borders and containers. Its radiant chartreuse leaves sparkle with purple-leaved *Strobilanthes dyerianus*, *Stachytarpheta jamaicensis*, and white-flowered *Hedychium coronarium*. Overwinters in zones 8–10.

Ensete ventricosum 'Maurelii'

RED-LEAF ABYSSINIAN BANANA

PRONOUNCED
en-SET-ee ven-trih-KO-sum

CARE NEEDS

IT'S ENOUGH TO make you believe in space aliens: how else do you explain a plant with leaves that grow six to fifteen feet long and three feet wide?!? Granted the foliage *only* reaches six feet when *Ensete* 'Maurelii' is grown as an annual, but that's still big enough to see it from outer space. Olive-green on their upper surfaces but burgundy underneath, the leaves glow wine-red when sunlit. Given rich soil and plentiful moisture, 'Maurelii' grows eight feet tall in one season. Span the textural spectrum—plant 'Maurelii' with *Hibiscus* 'Jungle Red', *Salvia* 'Van Houttei', *Duranta* 'Aurea', and *Solenostemon* 'Tiny Toes'. Overwinters in zones 9–10.

Euphorbia cotinifolia
TROPICAL SMOKEBUSH

PRONOUNCED
**you-FOR-bee-uh
kuh-ty-nih-FO-lee-uh**

CARE NEEDS

THOUGH IT RESEMBLES the tree known as purple smokebush (*Cotinus coggygria*), tropical smokebush is actually related to your holiday poinsettia! It's very different from that gaudy seasonal decoration, though. Its two-inch burgundy leaves are borne on slender red petioles, and as the sun shifts during the day its color changes from sultry wine to coppery red. Tropical smokebush is grown entirely for its elegant foliage; the tiny white flowers are scarcely noticeable. As an annual, it grows three feet tall, but if you can overwinter it indoors you will love its eventual treelike form, especially as backdrop to *Fuchsia* 'Gartenmeister Bonstedt' and *Acalypha* 'Obovata'. Overwinters in zones 9–10.

Euphorbia tirucalli 'Rosea'

STICKS-ON-FIRE FLAMING PENCIL TREE

PRONOUNCED
**you-FOR-bee-uh
teer-oo-KAL-eye**

CARE NEEDS

ODDLY BEAUTIFUL STICKS-ON-FIRE looks like a bizarre sculpture built of stubby little golf pencils—colored pencils, no less—in shades of chartreuse, soft orange, and watercolor red. Tiny matching leaves occasionally but in no predictable pattern assert themselves from the joints where the stems are joined. Grown as an annual, sticks-on-fire reaches eighteen inches tall during its first season. Overwinter it indoors, though; it's a long-lived plant that gets bigger and showier with age. Though it's drought resistant, sticks-on-fire grows faster with regular watering. Fun companions include *Acalypha* 'Cypress Elf', *Solenostemon* 'Aurora', *Cuphea ignea* peach-flowered form, and *Phormium* 'Atropurpureum'. Overwinters in zone 10.

Fuchsia triphylla 'Gartenmeister Bonstedt'

LADY'S EARRINGS

PRONOUNCED
FEW-shuh try-FILL-uh

CARE NEEDS

HUNDREDS OF FUCHSIA cultivars exist, each more exquisite than the last, but thirty-inch-tall *Fuchsia* 'Gartenmeister Bonstedt' rises above all others in at least one respect: heat tolerance. Its slender, deep coral blossoms hang in graceful, long-lasting clusters from upright stems—grown in shade, the flowers are a lovely, pale coral-orange. Small cranberry-like fruits follow the elegant blooms. Flowering slows in midsummer heat, but purple-tinged foliage, dark stems, and colorful berries carry the show until cooler days return. Then 'Gartenmeister Bonstedt' blooms its bonnet off until frost. Burgundy *Euphorbia cotinifolia* and *Impatiens repens* make splendid partners. Overwinters in zones 9–10.

Graptophyllum pictum 'Chocolate'

CHOCOLATE CARICATURE PLANT

PRONOUNCED
grap-toe-FILL-um PICK-tum

CARE NEEDS

GRAPTOPHYLLUM 'CHOCOLATE' BEARS sleek brown leaves centered with an irregular band of creamy sandstone pink. Its showy, shrimp-pink stems grow three feet tall in hot climates, one to two feet in cooler zones. Though its color is best in sun, 'Chocolate' accepts considerable shade; it even makes a good winter houseplant, which might allow you to see its cool-season, acanthus-like blossoms. Use 'Chocolate' as you would a coleus, though its growth will likely be slower. In sun, it looks scrumptious with *Pentas* 'Dorann's Pink' and *Alternanthera* calico form. In lightly shaded sites, replace 'Dorann's Pink' with *Fuchsia* 'Gartenmeister Bonstedt'. Overwinters in zones 9–10.

Hamelia patens

MEXICAN FIREBUSH

PRONOUNCED
huh-MEE-lee-uh PAY-tenz

CARE NEEDS

DO YOU NEED a plant that scoffs at heat, laughs at drought? Try Mexican firebush, which bears summer-to-frost clusters of scarlet-orange, tubular blossoms on thirty-inch stems. The flowers are followed by decorative red fruits that ripen blackberry-purple. Hummingbird-attracting blooms aren't its only virtue: Mexican firebush also boasts whorls of purple-tinged, high-gloss foliage held on rust-red stems. The more heat it receives, the better Mexican firebush flowers, so don't hesitate to plant it in your hottest spot. It makes a fiery show with burgundy *Pennisetum* 'Rubrum', *Oxalis spiralis* 'Aureus', and the giant wine-red leaves of purple castor bean, *Ricinus* 'Carmencita'. Overwinters in zones 9–10.

Hedychium coccineum var. aurantiacum 'Flaming Torch'

GINGER LILY

PRONOUNCED
huh-DICK-ee-um
cock-SIN-ee-um variety
or-an-tee-AY-kum

CARE NEEDS

SOME GINGER LILIES sprinkle their blossoms over a long season, but *Hedychium* 'Flaming Torch' holds aloft huge sconces that flare into bloom all at once in late summer. The entire cone ignites in a magnificent display of pale orange-chiffon petals with deep peach centers, and the two-tone color of the flowers gives the effect of flickering torches in the garden. Another pyrotechnic performance follows a few weeks after the first. Seven-foot-tall 'Flaming Torch' sports bold tropical foliage; like other ginger lilies, it performs best with ample water. It makes a winning combo with *Brugmansia* 'Sunset', peach-flowered *Cuphea ignea*, and burgundy *Euphorbia cotinifolia*. Overwinters in zones 7–10.

Hedychium coronarium

BUTTERFLY GINGER LILY

PRONOUNCED
**huh-DICK-ee-um
kore-uh-NAIR-ee-um**

CARE NEEDS

EVEN IF YOU only have room for ten tropical plants, you will need butterfly ginger lily. Its broad canna-like leaves on sturdy five-foot stalks provide a strong focal point among finer textures; then beginning in late summer and continuing until frost, three-inch flowers alight atop the stems like milky white butterflies. Oh, the fragrance! Part tropical sweetness, part spice, the scent rolls out into the heady heat of late afternoon. On warm nights you can revel in ginger lily's perfume from fifty feet away, enveloped in the silky essence of pure summer pleasure. *Breynia* 'Roseo-picta' and *Solenostemon* 'Mariposa' make exquisite companions. Overwinters in zones 7–10.

Hibiscus acetosella 'Jungle Red'

AFRICAN ROSE MALLOW

PRONOUNCED
huh-BISS-kus
uh-see-toe-SELL-uh

CARE NEEDS

TALL TROPICALS FORM the backdrop for summer beds and borders, and none are more elegant and graceful than *Hibiscus* 'Jungle Red'. Its wine-red, seven-foot stems bear lacy burgundy leaves resembling those of a Japanese maple. A single plant produces several stems held in an attractive vase shape; being slender at its base, it's easy to tuck smaller treasures underneath. If you overwinter 'Jungle Red' indoors, you'll see its leaves revert to their plainer winter shield-shape and observe the small, velvet-red blossoms that form in the leaf axils. Create a flamboyant combination with orange-flowered *Senecio confusus*, *Canna* 'Bengal Tiger', *Alternanthera* 'Red Threads', and green-and-gold *Alpinia zerumbet* 'Variegata'. Overwinters in zones 9–10.

Impatiens repens
CREEPING JEWELWEED

PRONOUNCED
im-PAY-shunz REE-penz

CARE NEEDS

AT FIRST GLANCE, gardeners sometimes reject creeping jewelweed in favor of more flamboyant plants (and because of the unfortunate word "weed" in its common name). A second look brings them around to its charms: delicate texture, subtle beauty, and a willingness to hug the ground or produce long swags of foliage that sway from containers. Creeping jewelweed's half-inch, somber green leaves and wine-red stems flatter almost any other color, making it handy for filling bare spots. Its shell-shaped golden flowers are sweet but not prolific. It makes a superb three-inch-tall groundcover underneath *Ensete* 'Maurelii', *Kalanchoe prolifera*, and burgundy *Salvia* 'Van Houttei'. Overwinter in zones 9–10.

Ipomoea batatas 'Margarita'

ORNAMENTAL SWEET POTATO

PRONOUNCED
ip-uh-MEE-uh buh-TAY-tus

CARE NEEDS

LOOKING FOR A radiant chartreuse tropical that takes scorching sun without burning and light shade without fading? *Ipomoea* 'Margarita' produces its colorful lemon-lime leaves on trailing stems that swiftly carpet several feet of border space once hot weather arrives. Its fast-moving stems barrel over shorter plants and sometimes shimmy up into taller ones, so choose companions that can take the competition. Drought-resistant 'Margarita' thrives in all but the heaviest soils—it's great for sandy sites and also for containers (even if you sometimes forget to water them). The lobed leaves have red-violet edges, a color echoed by *Strobilanthes dyerianus* and *Tibouchina urvilleana*. Overwinters in zones 9–10.

Ipomoea carnea subsp. fistulosa
TREE MORNING GLORY

PRONOUNCED
**ip-uh-MEE-uh
KAR-nee-uh subspecies
fist-you-LOW-suh**

CARE NEEDS

LOVE MORNING GLORIES, hate building trellises? Plant tree morning glory, which grows tall and straight on its own sturdy trunk. Quickly ascending to seven feet tall, tree morning glory sends forth clusters of pointed buds which unfurl into three-inch, lavender-pink flowers. The blossoms close by noon on hot days, but a new crop appears afresh every morning from midsummer until frost. Its attractive foliage is unscathed by powdery mildew, which disfigures vining morning glories in hot, humid climates. It's beautiful with *Musa basjoo*, *Saccharum* 'Pele's Smoke' and *Graptophyllum pictum* 'Chocolate'. Tree morning glory overwinters in zones 8b–10 but is unwelcome in zones 8b–11, where it is invasive from seed.

Iresine 'Purple Lady'

BLOODLEAF

PRONOUNCED
eye-riss-EYE-nee

CARE NEEDS

BURGUNDY FOLIAGE IS the basic black dress of the horticultural world: it can be planted almost anywhere, anytime. *Iresine* 'Purple Lady' brings that eminently useful color down to ankle height, forming a three-foot-wide, weed-suppressing carpet of crinkly inch-long leaves. Grown in containers, 'Purple Lady' drapes gracefully over the edges and interweaves with other trailing plants. Make a pretty potted trio with 'Purple Lady', *Sanchezia speciosa*, and red-and-yellow *Solenostemon* 'Tiny Toes'. For a larger space, plant 'Purple Lady' with purple-leaved *Ricinus* 'Carmencita', coral-striped *Canna* 'Phaison', *Xanthosoma* 'Lime Zinger', and *Fuchsia* 'Gartenmeister Bonstedt'. Overwinters in zones 9–10.

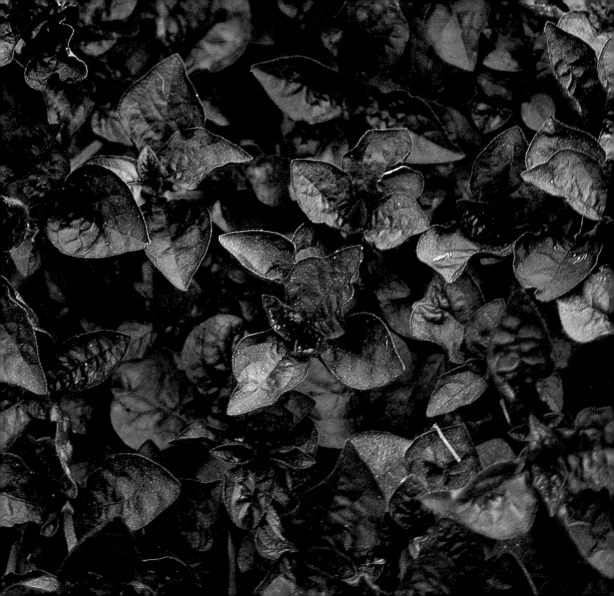

Kalanchoe prolifera
JURASSIC KALE

PRONOUNCED
**kuh-LANK-oh-ee
pro-LIFF-ur-uh**

CARE NEEDS

SWANK, HIP, AND PRIMITIVELY COOL, Jurassic kale's succulent, light green leaves jut from a thick, broccoli-like stalk that grows three feet or taller. It looks like lunch for a hungry chomposaurus munching its way through the forest primeval! Jurassic kale's leaves are edged in dark purple—a hint for choosing color echoes—and they occasionally form odd little protrusions that dangle like earrings from the leaf edges. (These mini-plantlets drop to the ground and root, making Jurassic kale potentially invasive in zones 9–11.) Its strong architectural lines contrast well with delicate trailers like *Impatiens repens*, *Iresine* 'Purple Lady', and *Petunia integrifolia*. Overwinters in zones 9–10 .

Lantana 'Desert Sunset'

PRONOUNCED
lan-TAN-uh

CARE NEEDS

LANTANA 'DESERT SUNSET' enlivens the garden with the radiant colors of a Mexican fiesta: vivid gold, peachy orange, saturated pink. The party continues without pause from summer to frost, providing a tasty feast for butterflies and a feast for the senses of color-hungry gardeners. Like other lantanas, three-foot-tall 'Desert Sunset' exhibits extreme drought resistance, though as long as it has decent soil drainage, rainy summers suit it, too. Rich green leaves make a brilliant foil for the profuse flower clusters, and 'Desert Sunset' also offers a pleasing rounded shape that stays tidy-looking all season. *Euphorbia tirucalli* 'Rosea' and pink-and-yellow *Cuphea cyanea* provide excellent companionship. Overwinters in zones 9–10.

Lantana 'Mozelle'

PRONOUNCED
lan-TAN-uh

CARE NEEDS

IT'S HARD TO imagine a plant more beautiful or generous with its blossoms than the exquisite *Lantana* 'Mozelle'. From late spring to frost, 'Mozelle' produces tiny rose-colored buds that open the soft yellow of newborn chicks, then deepen in color to rich rose-pink with a petite orange eye. As with other lantanas, its forest-green, fragrant foliage is impervious to pests and diseases and looks fresh all season. 'Mozelle' grows four feet tall on strong shrubby stems. It's at its best covered in nectar-sipping butterflies, but chocolate-colored *Saccharum* 'Pele's Smoke', dark rose *Salvia* 'Bethellii', and lemony *Tecoma stans* make pretty nice companions, too. Overwinters in zones 7b–10.

Lantana 'Pink Caprice'

PRONOUNCED
lan-TAN-uh

CARE NEEDS

THE TINY PILLOWCASE buds of *Lantana* 'Pink Caprice' begin life palest amber-pink. As they open the color shifts to soft lemon, then gradually goes pinker, until the petals arrive at last at a luscious shade of medium rose. The final color is much softer than dark pink *Lantana* 'Mozelle', but the shades are similar enough that they make gorgeous color echoes of one another. 'Pink Caprice' grows about thirty inches tall and wide, forming a rounded, shrubby mound of crisp green foliage. It's at its prettiest with other pastel plants, like *Canna* 'Constitution', icy lemon *Mirabilis* 'Baywatch', and the pale yellow form of *Tecomaria capensis*. Overwinters in zones 9–10.

Lantana 'Red Spread'

PRONOUNCED
lan-TAN-uh

CARE NEEDS

LANTANA 'RED SPREAD' sweeps the ground at twelve inches tall, spilling clusters of audacious red blooms that appear from late spring to frost. The tiny blossoms open deep gold but quickly change to the fiery red of ripe cayenne peppers. Low-growing 'Red Spread' has the same rich green, fragrant foliage of other lantanas, which makes a particularly handsome contrast to the saturated flower color. Once established, 'Red Spread' thrives in hot dry sites, even coastal sand, so don't be afraid to use it in your most daunting locations. Butterflies flock to 'Red Spread', which looks terrific with *Ricinus* 'Carmencita', *Salvia elegans*, and *Manihot esculenta* 'Variegata'. Overwinters in zones 9–10.

Manihot esculenta 'Variegata'

VARIEGATED TAPIOCA

PRONOUNCED
MAN-ih-hot ess-kew-LEN-tuh

CARE NEEDS

ONE OF THE world's most dazzling tropical foliage plants is also one of the toughest: meet *Manihot esculenta* 'Variegata', a plant so staunchly drought resistant it's used extensively in hot Texas landscapes. Its six-inch leaves resemble oversized maple foliage, except that each forest-green leaf is brushed with a central band of creamy yellow. A touch of red marks the leaf veins, and deep red petioles also contribute color. Three-foot-tall 'Variegata' makes a fast-growing, rounded mound; contrast its shape and color with giant *Ensete* 'Maurelii', burgundy *Salvia* 'Van Houttei', *Solenostemon* 'Tiny Toes', and *Alternanthera* 'Red Threads'. Overwinters in zones 9–10.

Mirabilis 'Baywatch'
GIANT FOUR O'CLOCK

PRONOUNCED
meer-AB-ih-liss

CARE NEEDS

IF YOU'RE FOND of simple pleasures, you probably already grow four o'clocks, but do you have one with champagne yellow, sweetly fragrant blossoms on *nine-foot stems*? That's right, *Mirabilis* 'Baywatch' grows six feet taller than most four o'clocks, bearing a new crop of flowers every evening from midsummer until frost. The blossoms open a little later than most four o'clocks, say around six p.m., announcing dinnertime for hummingbirds and night-flying sphinx moths that flock to their nectar. Rich soil produces the tallest plants, but even in sandy soil six feet is possible. 'Baywatch' looks beautiful with *Lantana* 'Mozelle', pale *Tecomaria capensis*, and towering *Musa basjoo*. Overwinters in zones 7–10.

Musa basjoo
HARDY BANANA

PRONOUNCED
MEW-zuh BAZ-joo

CARE NEEDS

STRETCH YOUR TEXTURAL palette to its limits with *Musa basjoo*, a hardy banana whose gigantic six-foot leaves make even cannas look small. Rocketing up to ten feet or taller, *Musa basjoo* is easy to grow if you provide fertile moist soil and plenty of elbow room. It thrives at the back of the border—or the front of the house!—or in large (okay, enormous) containers. To keep its leaves from shredding, avoid windy sites. To overwinter *Musa basjoo* in borderline hardy locations, bury its crown in three feet of coarse mulch. Build a tropical oasis with *Musa basjoo*, *Alocasia* 'Portodora', and *Crinum* 'Ellen Bosanquet'. Overwinters in zones 7–10.

Oplismenus hirtellus 'Variegatus'

VARIEGATED BASKET GRASS

PRONOUNCED
ah-PLIZ-mih-nus hur-TELL-us

CARE NEEDS

A QUICK GLANCE at its zigzag stems and trailing habit, and you'd swear that *Oplismenus* 'Variegatus' is a spiderwort in the genus *Tradescantia*. But it's a true grass whose nondescript autumn inflorescences pale beside its white, green, and magenta-pink foliage. 'Variegatus' creeps along the ground at flip-flop height, forming a three-foot patch of colorful two-inch leaves. Too bad it's not very hardy; wouldn't you love a tricolor lawn? Instead, plant a pretty container for sun with 'Variegatus', *Kalanchoe prolifera*, and magenta *Petunia integrifolia*. In shade, it makes a lovely underplanting for white-edged *Curcuma petiolata* 'Emperor'. Overwinters zones 9–10.

Oxalis spiralis 'Aureus'

GOLDEN FALSE CLOVER

PRONOUNCED
OCKS-uh-liss spih-RAL-iss

CARE NEEDS

DAINTY GOLDEN SHAMROCKS bedeck this delightful ground-cover or trailing container plant. In full sun, *Oxalis* 'Aureus' glows copper-gold, its half-inch leaflets rimmed in blush red and borne on reddish stems. Light shade turns the leaves to soft lime. Though it resembles clover, 'Aureus' bears tiny golden chalices instead of the rounded flower heads of true clover. It grows five inches tall and eighteen inches wide; it does not produce the underground bulblets that make some oxalis invasive. 'Aureus' shines in sun with *Euphorbia tirucalli* 'Rosea' and *Salvia* 'Caribbean Coral'; in shade, grow it with *Fuchsia* 'Gartenmeister Bonstedt' and *Plectranthus* 'Green on Green'. Overwinters in zones 9–10.

Pennisetum macrostachyum 'Burgundy Giant'

GIANT FOUNTAIN GRASS

PRONOUNCED
**pen-ih-SEE-tum
mack-ro-STAY-kee-um**

CARE NEEDS

WHEN A PLANTING calls for a grassy backdrop, *Pennisetum* 'Burgundy Giant' answers with startling red foliage on stiff wine-dark stalks. Closely related to burgundy fountain grass (*Pennisetum setaceum* 'Rubrum'), five-foot-tall 'Burgundy Giant' is the upright counterpart to its weeping cousin. It keeps its alluring foliage color all season—your neighbors will think you're growing a crop of narrow-leaved burgundy corn! The bushy plumes that top the stems age from wine-red to the color of your morning Wheaties. Orange *Hamelia patens* and *Canna* 'Phaison' glow against the dramatically dark foliage of 'Burgundy Giant', or create a red-and-gold combo with *Alpinia* 'Variegata', *Ensete* 'Maurelii', and *Lantana* 'Red Spread'. Overwinters in zones 8b–10.

Pennisetum setaceum 'Rubrum'
BURGUNDY FOUNTAIN GRASS

PRONOUNCED
**pen-ih-SEE-tum
seh-TAY-see-um**

CARE NEEDS

PENNISETUM 'RUBRUM' IS a Top Ten tropical, a gotta-have grass famous in the gardening world for its dark burgundy blades that form an arching fountain of color. Fast-growing 'Rubrum' makes a lush, three-foot-tall showpiece, and all season long it bears smoky purple plumes that slowly age to tan. The inflorescences are handsome at any stage, both in the garden and in cutflower bouquets. Though it grows faster in moist soil, built-in drought resistance explains why 'Rubrum' succeeds in inhospitable sites like shopping mall parking lots. For a superb red combination, pair 'Rubrum' with *Salvia splendens* 'Van Houttei', *Ensete* 'Maurelii', and *Alternanthera* 'Red Threads'. Overwinters in zones 8b–10.

Pentas lanceolata 'Dorann's Pink'

STAR CLUSTER

PRONOUNCED
PEN-tus lan-see-oh-LAY-tuh

CARE NEEDS

IF THE ONLY pentas you've seen are little six-inch bedding blobs that come in insipid pastel colors, you'd never know there were tall, floriferous selections of pentas in knock-you-sideways shades. A respectable eighteen inches tall, *Pentas* 'Dorann's Pink' blooms from summer to frost, bearing clusters of starry, hot pink flowers that edge toward coral, centered with violet-pink eyes. The petal coloring suggests combinations with plants in sunset shades, like *Solenostemon* 'Aurora', *Lantana* 'Desert Sunset', and *Euphorbia tirucalli* 'Rosea'. Magic happens when you add chocolate-colored *Canna* 'Constitution' and *Saccharum* 'Pele's Smoke'. You may have to brush eager butterflies away from the flowers to see them yourself! Overwinters in zones 9–10.

Petunia integrifolia
WILD PETUNIA

PRONOUNCED
**peh-TOON-yuh
in-teg-rih-FO-lee-uh**

CARE NEEDS

TASTEFUL GARDENERS USED to spurn "tacky" colors like magenta, consigning it to the ranks of tire planters, dinner-plate dahlias, and other forms of garden fun—that is, until they noticed that the magnificent color of *Petunia integrifolia* revives pastel plantings bleached to insignificance by strong summer sun. Its small, black-eyed blossoms never look scraggly, even in rainy weather. In hot, humid climates, it's the only petunia that still looks great (or even alive) by autumn. *Petunia integrifolia* grows three feet wide, and its height is determined by surrounding plants, because this sticky-stemmed petunia sometimes scrambles into its bordermates. It's gorgeous with silver-leaved *Centaurea* 'Colchester White' and *Strobilanthes dyerianus*. Overwinters in zones 8–10.

Phormium tenax 'Atropurpureum'
NEW ZEALAND FLAX

PRONOUNCED
FORE-mee-um TEN-acks

CARE NEEDS

PHORMIUMS TYPICALLY DESPISE hot, humid weather and do best in cool-summer climates, but at last there's one that also tolerates sultry southern extremes: *Phormium* 'Atropurpureum', which produces sword-shaped leaves in a clump that resembles yucca (minus the nasty sharp points). Where it overwinters, 'Atropurpureum' makes a dramatic sculptural mass whose chocolate-purple leaves grow three to five feet long. Treated as an annual, it can be expected to reach two feet tall. Like other phormiums, 'Atropurpureum' appreciates good soil drainage. Hate having to water your containers every single day? Combine drought-resistant 'Atropurpureum' with pink-and-yellow *Cuphea cyanea* and *Euphorbia tirucalli* 'Rosea'. They will almost grow without you! Overwinters in zones 7b–10.

Plectranthus argentatus

SILVER SPURFLOWER

PRONOUNCED
**pleck-TRAN-thus
ar-jun-TAY-tus**

CARE NEEDS

TRUST THE TROPICS to deliver a silver-leaved plant that doesn't rot in humid summer climates. Looking rather like a lofty version of hardy lamb's ears (*Stachys byzantina*), *Plectranthus argentatus* bears its downy silver-green leaves on three-foot, mauve-tinted stems. Its habit resembles that of coleus, its tropical cousin. Square stems indicate membership in the mint family, but don't worry, *Plectranthus argentatus* won't stage an underground takeover. Formidably drought resistant, it also thrives in monsoon summers, growing bigger and more beautiful no matter what challenges the growing season presents. Stellar companions include variegated hot pepper (*Capsicum annuum*), *Salvia* 'Waverly', and *Solenostemon* 'Blackberry Waffles'. Overwinters in zones 9–10.

Plectranthus coleoides

WHITE EDGED SWEDISH IVY

PRONOUNCED
**pleck-TRAN-thus
ko-lee-oh-EYE-deez**

CARE NEEDS

A PLANT OF multiple personalities, *Plectranthus coleoides* is as at home in hot, dry sites as it is in lightly shaded, moist soil. A shrubby-looking plant that grows eighteen inches tall and wide, it produces two-tone, sage-green leaves ringed in milky white. In full sun, it has two-inch leaves and a tight, rounded habit, while in shade it takes on a more relaxed, open aspect. Like other members of its genus, *Plectranthus coleoides* has never heard of inclement weather—nothing fazes it but frost. It makes an elegant companion to white-flowered *Hedychium coronarium*, pink-and-white *Breynia* 'Roseo-picta', and pink *Ipomoea carnea* subsp. *fistulosa*. Overwinters in zones 9–10.

Plectranthus forsteri 'Green on Green'
SPURFLOWER

PRONOUNCED
pleck-TRAN-thus FOR-stur-eye

CARE NEEDS

STRONG, SUBSTANTIVE, AND nigh indestructible, *Plectranthus* 'Green on Green' produces downy leaves of soft apple green edged in pale chartreuse. The delicacy of its coloring belies a mighty tolerance for weather extremes: from drought to drowning weather, 'Green on Green' keeps its suave appearance until frost. Its stout, thirty-inch stems and thick, three-inch leaves provide a sturdy presence among fluffier textures, while its soft color enhances many other shades. Contrast 'Green on Green' with orange *Cuphea* 'David Verity' and the coffee-colored foliage of *Pseuderanthemum atropurpureum*; or create an old-fashioned, faded-postcard effect with red-and-yellow *Abutilon* 'Little Imp' and the strawberry catkins of *Acalypha pendula*. Overwinters in zones 9–10.

Plectranthus madagascariensis 'Marginatus'
VARIEGATED MINT-LEAF

PRONOUNCED
pleck-TRAN-thus
mad-uh-gas-kar-ee-EN-siss

CARE NEEDS

IN THE HOTTEST days of summer, it's thrilling to find a plant that looks as cool and happy as *Plectranthus* 'Marginatus'. A tricolor blend of crisp white, mint, and sage green, 'Marginatus' bears its fragrant inch-wide leaves on soft purple, three-foot stems. Its spring-fresh foliage never falters, no matter what the weather. 'Marginatus' grows in sun or light shade and makes a superlative two-inch-tall groundcover or trailing plant for containers. Plant a sweep underneath white-edged *Curcuma* 'Emperor' and *Colocasia fallax* in shady sites; or let 'Marginatus' tumble from a sunny container with *Solenostemon* 'Mariposa' and *Colocasia* 'Black Magic'. Overwinters in zones 9–10.

Pseuderanthemum atropurpureum
BLACK-LEAF SHOOTING STAR

PRONOUNCED
**soo-dur-AN-thuh-mum
at-ro-pur-PUR-ee-um**

CARE NEEDS

DARK AS THE sky in the single-digit hours of the morning, rich as the strongest cup of coffee you've ever tasted, black-leaf shooting star draws every eye to its fathomless depths. A three-foot column of burnished bronze-black leaves, it forms a weighty visual anchor that enhances almost any color. Black-leaf shooting star produces the occasional starry white blossom, but with a foliage show like this, who needs flowers? It looks sexy with *Centaurea* 'Colchester White' and rose-red *Crinum* 'Ellen Bosanquet'; sultry with orange *Cuphea* 'David Verity' and fiery *Canna* 'Phaison'; and startling with chartreuse *Duranta* 'Aurea' and *Xanthosoma* 'Lime Zinger'. Overwinters in zones 9–10.

Ricinus communis 'Carmencita'

CASTOR BEAN

PRONOUNCED
RISS-ih-niss kum-YOU-niss

CARE NEEDS

FROM A BEAN-SIZED seed, *Ricinus* 'Carmencita' propels itself skyward, forming a robust eight- to twelve-foot tower of wine-red stems and burgundy maple-like leaves up to two feet across. Uninspiring creamy blooms appear with little fanfare in late summer, but the subsequent seedpods are astonishing: eight-inch spikes of either chocolate or coral-red pods that resemble walnut-sized sea anemones. Both forms are gorgeous and produce plentiful seed for next year. (Warning: plants and seeds are considered poisonous.) For best results, direct-sow the seeds into loose rich soil after frost has passed. 'Carmencita' makes a spectacular backdrop for hot-striped *Canna* 'Phaison', *Xanthosoma* 'Lime Zinger', and *Cuphea* 'David Verity'. Overwinters in zones 8b–10.

Saccharum officinarum 'Pele's Smoke'

CHOCOLATE SUGARCANE

PRONOUNCED
**SACK-ur-um
uh-fiss-ih-NAIR-um**

CARE NEEDS

LUSCIOUS, ALLURING *SACCHARUM* 'Pele's Smoke' is an eight- to twelve-foot-tall grass whose dusky plum canes sport chocolate-purple leaves, many with a long pink mid-rib. Being a true sugarcane—though alas not chocolate flavored—'Pele's Smoke' prefers rich, moist soil. Otherwise, it's easy to please and grows faster than Jack's beanstalk when summer heat hits. A single cane looks lonely, though, so group several stems per planting hole. One hot combo joins 'Pele's Smoke' with chocolate-and-coral *Acalypha* 'Obovata' and *Salvia* 'Caribbean Coral'; or play to its sweeter side, with fuchsia-pink *Salvia* 'Bethellii', *Breynia* 'Roseo-picta', *Ipomoea carnea* subsp. *fistulosa*, and pink-and-cream *Ananas comosus* 'Variegatus'. Overwinters in zones 9–10.

Salvia elegans
PINEAPPLE SAGE

PRONOUNCED
SAL-vee-uh EL-ih-ganz

CARE NEEDS

FRAGRANT FOLIAGE EARNS pineapple sage its common name: the fruity scent is reminiscent of pineapple, and the leaves make a tasty tea. Pineapple sage is at its radiant best in late summer and fall, when the four-foot stems are topped with hummingbird-attracting, tubular red blossoms. It grows fastest in average-to-rich soil that receives regular watering, but pineapple sage is fairly drought resistant in a pinch. As with other salvias, leaving dead stems standing until early spring increases the odds of winter survival. Pineapple sage sizzles with burgundy-leaved *Ricinus* 'Carmencita' and *Alternanthera* 'Red Threads', or plant it as a backdrop for purple-flowered *Tibouchina urvilleana*. Overwinters in zones 8–10.

Salvia
'Indigo Spires'

PRONOUNCED
SAL-vee-uh

CARE NEEDS

SALVIA '**INDIGO SPIRES**' blooms from early summer to frost, its two-inch, blue-purple blossoms held in indigo bracts. As cool late-season temperatures arrive, the flowers deepen to the blue of a bottomless lake. 'Indigo Spires' has another special feature: its ever-elongating flower spikes develop wonderful swooping curves, until by late summer the roller-coaster stems reach up to three feet long. 'Indigo Spires' grows three feet tall and four feet wide in hot climates; it's smaller and later to bloom in cooler regions. Like many salvias, it overwinters best in well-drained locations. White-flowered *Hedychium coronarium*, *Pentas* 'Dorann's Pink', and *Solenostemon* 'Mariposa' make vibrant companions. Overwinters in 7–10.

Salvia involucrata 'Bethellii'

ROSEBUD SAGE

PRONOUNCED
SAL-vee-uh
in-voll-you-KRAY-tuh

CARE NEEDS

THE SMALL SATIN buds of *Salvia* 'Bethellii' are round as a baby's cheeks and open to reveal inch-long, fuchsia-pink blossoms held in plum-pink bracts. Plum tints highlight the leaf veins and petioles, too. 'Bethellii' grows three to six feet tall and blooms from late summer until frost. As with many tropical salvias, it grows larger in hot climates with earlier spring planting dates. Though its stems are strong, late-summer storms occasionally spill 'Bethellii' sideways, so provide tall, structural partners like *Ricinus* 'Carmencita' or *Saccharum* 'Pele's Smoke'. Other handsome companions include *Colocasia* 'Black Magic', *Lantana* 'Pink Caprice', and lemony *Tecomaria capensis*. Overwinters in zones 9–10.

Salvia leucantha
MEXICAN BUSH SAGE

PRONOUNCED
SAL-vee-uh loo-KAN-thuh

CARE NEEDS

FROM THE FIRST moment, you recognize that the sage-green, willowy leaves and woolly white stems of Mexican bush sage are something special. As it grows, bush sage becomes even more beautiful, until by late summer you think you wouldn't care if it never flowered. But it does, beginning in September, with eighteen-inch spikes of sparkling white blossoms that protrude from fuzzy red-violet bracts. It blooms until a hard freeze sends it into dormancy (or to the Great Green Hereafter). Five-foot-tall Mexican bush sage is drought resistant and prefers good soil drainage. Pair it with white-flowered *Hedychium coronarium* and purple-leaved *Strobilanthes dyerianus*. Overwinters in zones 7–10.

Salvia mexicana 'Limelight'

PRONOUNCED
SAL-vee-uh mecks-ih-KAY-nuh

CARE NEEDS

SALVIA 'LIMELIGHT' IS a beauty from spring to frost, but especially beginning in late August when its showy chartreuse flower bracts begin to form. Four weeks later, when deep blue tubular blossoms emerge from the jazzy bracts, the contrast is stunning. Five-foot-tall 'Limelight' flowers for months in the low light levels of fall and winter (or until hard frost). All season long, it provides seductive silvery-green stems cloaked in dark, satiny foliage etched with pale veins. 'Limelight' tolerates drought but prefers moisture-retentive soils. *Ipomoea* 'Margarita' and *Xanthosoma* 'Lime Zinger' echo its chartreuse bracts, or combine it with *Hedychium coronarium* and silver *Plectranthus argentatus*. Overwinters in 8b–10.

Salvia splendens 'Caribbean Coral'

PRONOUNCED
SAL-vee-uh SPLEN-denz

CARE NEEDS

YOU MAY ALREADY be growing the compact forms of *Salvia splendens* known as scarlet bedding sage—did you know there were tall, elegant selections available as well? For years, only one was known: burgundy-colored 'Van Houttei'. Then suddenly other lofty forms appeared, including the magnificent *Salvia* 'Caribbean Coral'. In bloom from early summer to frost, three-foot-tall 'Caribbean Coral' produces iridescent coral-orange blossoms streaked with shrimp-pink. The hummingbird-attracting blooms are borne in long-lasting orange bracts. 'Caribbean Coral' sparkles in sunlight with *Hedychium* 'Flaming Torch', *Acalypha* 'Cypress Elf', and chocolate-purple *Phormium* 'Atropurpureum'. Electrify shady sites with 'Caribbean Coral' and *Begonia carolinifolia*. Overwinters in zones 9–10.

Salvia splendens 'Van Houttei'

ALSO SOLD AS
Salvia van houttii

PRONOUNCED
SAL-vee-uh SPLEN-denz,
SAL-vee-uh van HOW-tee-eye

CARE NEEDS

FROM EARLY SUMMER until frost, *Salvia* 'Van Houttei' produces swan-necked flower spikes that straighten as they begin to bloom, unveiling burgundy-tinged-scarlet blossoms that weep from wine-red bracts. The long-lasting bracts retain their color even after the flowers have fallen. Planted out after spring frost, 'Van Houttei' rapidly rises to three feet or taller. Its luxuriant color is the garden equivalent of a crushed-velvet Cleopatra couch; pair it with other saturated shades or use 'Van Houttei' to enrich a planting of pastels. *Duranta erecta* 'Aurea', *Xanthosoma* 'Lime Zinger', and red Abyssinian banana, *Ensete* 'Maurelii', make radiant companions. Overwinters in zones 9–10.

Salvia 'Waverly'

PRONOUNCED
SAL-vee-uh

CARE NEEDS

LIKE TINY PRISMS struck by sunlight, the white-blushed-lavender blossoms of *Salvia* 'Waverly' twinkle atop four-foot branches cloaked in deep green, linear leaves. The fuzzy, half-inch flowers are held in purple-tinted bracts and resemble the blooms of Mexican bush sage (*Salvia leucantha*), a likely parent of this mysterious hybrid which appeared in gardening circles several years ago. 'Waverly' isn't stiffly upright like bush sage, though; it has a more relaxed presence, its strong stems spreading outward to four feet wide. In flower from early summer to frost, 'Waverly' creates a scintillating scene when partnered with purple *Strobilanthes dyerianus* and *Centaurea* 'Colchester White'. Overwinters in zones 8–10.

Sanchezia speciosa
SHRUBBY GOLD-VEIN

PRONOUNCED
san-CHEZZ-ee-uh
spee-see-OH-suh

CARE NEEDS

WITH THEIR HAPHAZARD blotches and spots, some variegated plants look like Jackson Pollock paintings. The exquisite foliage of *Sanchezia speciosa* was created by a master craftsman, though, not some abstract paint slinger. It took a keen eye and steady hand to apply the golden brush strokes that accent sanchezia's leaf veins and margins. And who but a genius would have added ruby stems? Imaginative gardeners might credit Leonardo da Vinci with inventing three-foot-tall sanchezia, which makes a picture-perfect focal point for borders and containers. Leo probably liked it with burgundy *Salvia* 'Van Houttei' and the red catkins of *Acalypha pendula*. Overwinters in zones 9–10.

Senecio confusus
MEXICAN FLAME VINE
ORANGEGLOW VINE

ALSO SOLD AS
Pseudogynoxys chenopodioides

PRONOUNCED
**suh-NEE-see-oh kun-FEW-zus,
soo-doe-jy-NOCKS-iss
kee-no-po-dee-oh-EYE-deez**

CARE NEEDS

WANT A VINE that gently weaves through other plants, instead of throttling them with its strangling stems? Mexican flame vine scrambles through its bordermates or container companions, scattering clusters of hot orange, two-inch daisies that appear from summer to frost. Glossy green, toothed leaves make a handsome backdrop for its three-alarm flowers. Used as an annual, Mexican flame vine grows six feet or taller if you tie it to a trellis, or let it hitch its own ride as it wanders among orange-flowered *Canna* 'Bengal Tiger', *Solenostemon* 'Blackberry Waffles', and purple-variegated *Capsicum annuum*. Overwinters in zone 10.

Senna didymotropa
POPCORN BUSH

PRONOUNCED
SEN-uh did-ih-mo-**TRO**-puh

CARE NEEDS

IT'S HARD TO work around popcorn bush near meal time—its fresh-popped fragrance will have you heading for the kitchen! The aromatic foliage is surprisingly elegant for such a movies-and-football-games smell: picture fifteen-inch-long leaves composed of paired oval leaflets, borne on a statuesque, upright plant. Crowning the five-foot stems in late summer are spires of buttery-yellow blossoms that spring from glossy brown buds. Contrast the dainty texture of drought-tolerant popcorn bush with the gigantic leaves of *Musa basjoo* or *Ricinus* 'Carmencita'; echo its lovely flowers with *Lantana* 'Desert Sunset' and the gold-and-green foliage of *Manihot esculenta* 'Variegata'. Overwinters in zones 9–10.

Solanum quitoense
BED-OF-NAILS
NARANJILLA

PRONOUNCED
suh-LAY-num kee-toe-EN-see

CARE NEEDS

"WHAT ON EARTH is that plant with the huge leaves and OH-MY-GOSH-THORNS?" From delight to horror, bed-of-nails provokes a sharp reaction from gardeners. Its olive-green leaves grow almost two feet across, and they're held in horizontal fashion, the better to see the inch-long purple spines protruding from the leaf veins. The new leaves of bed-of-nails are covered in downy purple fuzz, while older ones still sport a fine velvet stubble. White flowers tucked tight against the thorny, thirty-inch-tall trunk give way to fuzzy green fruits that ripen to pale pumpkin-orange. Burgundy *Euphorbia cotinifolia*, *Lantana* 'Red Spread', and *Pennisetum setaceum* 'Rubrum' make cozy bedfellows. Overwinters in zone 10.

Solenostemon 'Aurora'

COLEUS

PRONOUNCED
suh-leen-uh-STEE-mun

CARE NEEDS

PERHAPS THE LOVELIEST coleus you will ever grow, *Solenostemon* 'Aurora' has opalescent cream-colored leaves bathed in a watercolor wash of pale pink. The edges are brushed with green, while the leaf undersides are soft sunset pink. On all but the cloudiest days, the soft pink shines through the upper surface of the foliage, illuminating it from beneath. Two-foot-tall *Solenostemon* 'Aurora' boasts stocky stems and short internodes which give it a full, rounded form. Buttery *Tecomaria capensis*, soft orange *Hedychium* 'Flaming Torch', and the chocolate, cream, and pink leaves of *Talipariti tiliaceum* 'Tricolor' make lovely partners for the sunset shades of 'Aurora'. Overwinters in zones 9–10.

Solenostemon 'Blackberry Waffles'

COLEUS

PRONOUNCED
suh-leen-uh-STEE-mun

CARE NEEDS

WHAT A PERFECT name for a coleus with puckered leaves the silky purple color of blackberry syrup! With thirty-inch stems as dark as its foliage, *Solenostemon* 'Blackberry Waffles' anchors pastel plantings bleached by summer sun and provides a saturated backdrop to sizzling colors like orange and red. Like other coleus, 'Blackberry Waffles' produces its best color in evenly moist, average-to-rich soil—avoid drought or overfertilization, both of which turn coleus colors dull. *Canna* 'Bengal Tiger', orange *Senecio confusus*, and *Cuphea* 'David Verity' make incandescent partners; or pair 'Blackberry Waffles' with magenta *Petunia integrifolia*, pink-striped *Oplismenus* 'Variegatus', and tree morning glory, *Ipomoea carnea* subsp. *fistulosa*. Overwinters in zones 9–10.

Solenostemon 'Fishnet Stockings'

COLEUS

PRONOUNCED
suh-leen-uh-STEE-mun

CARE NEEDS

IF YOU'VE EVER seen a frog in fishnet stockings, you have a clue what this sexy new coleus looks like! Each and every vein of its chubby, rounded leaves is painted with a thick line of black-purple, set against a backdrop of vibrant frog-green (or bright lime, if you aren't into amphibians). The scalloped leaf edges of *Solenostemon* 'Fishnet Stockings' are inked as well, while a black blotch marks the base of each leaf. Its coloring goes great with anything, but two-foot-tall 'Fishnet Stockings' particularly likes to paint the town green with *Colocasia* 'Illustris' and trailing green-and-white *Plectranthus madagascariensis* 'Marginatus'. Overwinters in zones 9–10.

Solenostemon 'Mariposa'
COLEUS

PRONOUNCED
suh-leen-uh-STEE-mun

CARE NEEDS

ALONG WITH ALL the swallowtails, monarchs, and other butterflies that glorify the world, there ought to exist this beautiful mariposa (Spanish for butterfly). It would have gorgeous crimson wings, scalloped along the edges. The crimson would glow with tints of orange and pink that deepen to nearly black at the center. This fantasy butterfly would be huge, with a single wing reaching four, six, even eight inches long. Alas, *Solenostemon* 'Mariposa' isn't a butterfly, but it is the next best thing, a beautiful thirty-inch-tall coleus that can alight in your garden with *Breynia* 'Roseo-picta', *Colocasia* 'Black Magic', and *Iresine* 'Purple Lady'. Overwinters in 9–10.

Solenostemon 'New Hurricane'

COLEUS

PRONOUNCED
suh-leen-uh-STEE-mun

CARE NEEDS

YOU'LL BE BLOWN away by *Solenostemon* 'New Hurricane', one of the best and most bizarre coleus ever invented. Its wild-looking leaves are predominantly red, edged in lemon-yellow and sometimes centered with green. Short internodes produce tight, compact growth that gives two-foot-tall 'New Hurricane' an almost shrubby look. Like most modern coleus, it excels in sun but also thrives in light shade. Incorporate 'New Hurricane' into your perennial borders, where its intense color and texture will provide excitement long after flowering perennials have faded. Or combine it with other tropicals, like wine-red *Euphorbia cotinifolia*, *Salvia* 'Van Houttei', lemony *Tecoma stans*, and *Solenostemon* 'Tiny Toes'. Overwinters in zones 9–10.

Solenostemon 'Religious Radish'
COLEUS

PRONOUNCED
suh-leen-uh-STEE-mun

CARE NEEDS

SO WHAT WILL the originator of 'Religious Radish' name his next coleus, 'Secular Swiss Cheese'? Luckily, it's not just the wacky name that makes *Solenostemon* 'Religious Radish' a must-have: it's a beauty, whether grown in borders or containers, sanctified soil or regular garden dirt. Its near-black, six-inch leaves are edged in radish red, and they hold their color all season long, even in extreme heat. Like most coleus, when grown in light shade the leaves are both larger and paler in color. Thirty-inch-tall 'Religious Radish' makes a perfect partner for dark-leaved *Canna* 'Australia', *Colocasia* 'Black Magic', burgundy *Salvia* 'Van Houttei', and *Solenostemon* 'Tiny Toes'. Overwinters in zones 9–10.

Solenostemon 'Tiny Toes'

COLEUS

PRONOUNCED
suh-leen-uh-STEE-mun

CARE NEEDS

SOLENOSTEMON 'TINY TOES' is a textural delight, one of the most petite and unusual coleus you'll find. Its eight-inch stems are crowded with spoon-shaped, red-centered leaves edged in lemon-lime. They look like wiggly Martian toes painted with red polish! Even the largest leaves are only an inch long, yet the stems are so tightly packed with foliage that they create a dense, colorful mound eight inches tall and eighteen inches wide. 'Tiny Toes' belongs at the front of the border or in containers, where its delicacy can be appreciated. *Duranta* 'Aurea' and *Sanchezia speciosa* echo its cheerful coloring. Overwinters in zones 9–10.

Stachytarpheta jamaicensis

SMUGGLER'S VERVAIN

PORTERWEED

PRONOUNCED
**stack-ee-tar-FEET-uh
juh-may-KEN-siss**

CARE NEEDS

CREATE A COLORFUL garden scrim with smuggler's vervain, whose whiplike flower spikes rise into the air like enchanted green snakes, bearing violet-red flowers that sparkle with color. The verbena-like blossoms open over several weeks, blooming from bottom to top along the eighteen-inch spikes. Smuggler's vervain is always in bloom, a boon to local butterflies. Its foliage is attractive, too: soft green, felted four-inch leaves with a handsome quilted appearance. Four-foot-tall smuggler's vervain looks lovely with purple *Strobilanthes dyerianus*, sunny yellow *Tecoma stans*, and white-flowered *Hedychium coronarium*. Smuggler's vervain overwinters in zones 9–10, but is considered invasive from seed in zones 9–11.

Strobilanthes dyerianus
PERSIAN SHIELD

PRONOUNCED
**stro-bih-LAN-theez
die-ur-ee-AY-nus**

CARE NEEDS

GARDENERS GASP LIKE delighted children when they first see Persian shield, amazed that such metallic red-violet foliage exists. The leaves shimmer with a reflective silvery sheen that contrasts with the deep green leaf veins. Colors are most intense on younger foliage; older leaves pale to pink and shining silver. Like most tropicals, Persian shield lacks a cold-protective dormancy signal; instead it goes on producing shiny new seven-inch leaves until frost. In sunny gardens, partner thirty-inch tall Persian shield with *Salvia* 'Waverly', *Centaurea* 'Colchester White', and *Hedychium coronarium*. In sun or shade, try it with *Xanthosoma* 'Lime Zinger' and *Ipomoea* 'Margarita'. Overwinters in zones 8b–10.

Talipariti tiliaceum 'Tricolor'

SEA HIBISCUS
VARIEGATED
HAU TREE

ALSO SOLD AS
Hibiscus tiliaceus

PRONOUNCED
tal-ih-PAIR-ih-tee
til-ee-AY-see-um

huh-BISS-kus til-ee-AY-see-us

CARE NEEDS

A SUDDEN SEA change has shifted *Talipariti* 'Tricolor' from its old home in the hibiscus family, but it retains its claim to fame: broad leathery leaves that emerge deep reddish brown splashed with shrimp pink, then slowly age to green, pale pink, and creamy white. A tree in its native tropics, 'Tricolor' grows four feet tall and three feet wide when used as an annual. It's a shy bloomer in temperate climates, but when it does flower, 'Tricolor' produces golden blossoms that redden by sunset. It prefers evenly moist soil and looks stunning with *Saccharum* 'Pele's Smoke' and *Lantana* 'Pink Caprice'. Overwinters in zones 9b–10.

Tecoma stans
TROPICAL YELLOW BELLS
TRUMPET BUSH

PRONOUNCED
tuh-KO-muh STANZ

CARE NEEDS

COMBINING BEAUTY WITH exquisite fragrance, tropical yellow bells produces ruffled, daffodil-yellow blossoms sweetened with a fresh-baked-cookies fragrance. The summer-to-frost flower clusters appear above vibrant green, pinnate leaves that make a gorgeous backdrop for the two-inch blooms. Where it overwinters, yellow bells can become a twenty-foot shrub. Treated as an annual, it grows four feet tall and produces sturdy, self-supporting growth. Yellow bells is drought resistant once established; it also tolerates coastal wind and salt spray. Partner it with violet-red *Stachytarpheta jamaicensis* and *Strobilanthes dyerianus,* or create a sugar-sweet combo with *Saccharum* 'Pele's Smoke' and *Lantana* 'Pink Caprice'. Overwinters in zones 9–10.

Tecomaria capensis — pale yellow form

YELLOW CAPE HONEYSUCKLE

PRONOUNCED
teck-oh-MAIR-ee-uh
kuh-PEN-siss

CARE NEEDS

YOU MAY ALREADY be growing the molten-orange form of cape honeysuckle—harder to find is this icy lemon selection, whose clusters of ethereal blossoms seem to cool the surrounding air on hot late-summer days. The two-inch flowers continue well into autumn, providing elegant contrast to fall's pyrotechnic leaf display. All season long you'll enjoy cape honeysuckle's glossy green, pinnate leaves, which ascend shrubby four-foot stems. Contrast its lacy texture with the bold foliage of butterfly ginger lily (*Hedychium coronarium*); then add *Mirabilis* 'Baywatch', dainty pink-and-yellow *Lantana* 'Mozelle', and for a shot of saturated color, crimson-pink *Solenostemon* 'Mariposa'. Overwinters in zones 9–10.

Thunbergia battescombei
KING'S GLORY

PRONOUNCED
thoon-BURG-ee-uh
bat-iss-KOME-bee-eye

CARE NEEDS

A SCANDENT SHRUB or sprawling vine, king's glory sends its wandering stems scrambling through other plants, bedecking them with royal purple blossoms. Radiant golden throats accent the three-inch flowers, which grow singly or in loose clusters among glossy green leaves on lax three-foot stems. Nudge it up a trellis, send it weaving through the border, or let king's glory trail over the edges of containers, where it will lift its flowers up to greet viewers. King's glory looks quite tropical, yet it often overwinters in parts of zones 7. Golden *Canna* 'Bengal Tiger' and *Duranta* 'Aurea' make excellent partners. Overwinters in zones 7b–10.

Thunbergia grandiflora

BLUE SKY VINE

PRONOUNCED
thoon-BURG-ee-uh
gran-dih-FLOR-uh

CARE NEEDS

WINGED BLOSSOMS TAKE flight as blue sky vine ascends trellises, arbors, or other strong supports, rapidly growing up to ten feet tall. The sky-blue, three-inch flowers appear singly or in clusters from late summer to frost, displayed against attractive seven-inch leaves. Blue sky vine prefers reliable moisture and average-to-rich soil; where it's hardy, it may grow fifty feet tall. White and yellow markings in the flowers' throats suggest color echoes with *Hedychium coronarium* and *Xanthosoma* 'Albomarginatum'; or contrast blue sky vine's pastel shades with orange-chiffon *Hedychium* 'Flaming Torch' and pale peach *Brugmansia* 'Sunset'. Overwinters in zones 9b–10.

Tibouchina urvilleana

PRINCESS FLOWER

GLORY BUSH

PRONOUNCED
tib-oo-KY-nuh
ur-vil-ee-AY-nuh

CARE NEEDS

THE BLOSSOMS ARE captivating: regal purple and three inches across, their five silken petals surround flirty purple stamens that resemble long curled eyelashes. The flowers swirl open from fuzzy, red-tinged buds and appear from midsummer until frost. You'll be tempted to buy princess flower before you ever see it bloom, though, attracted by its downy green leaves lit by silvery hairs. Older leaves eventually turn soft scarlet before falling. A sturdy four-foot shrub, princess flower can be easily trained into a single-stemmed standard. It makes a stunning container specimen with a sweep of strawberry-red *Acalypha pendula* or chartreuse *Ipomoea* 'Margarita' at its feet. Overwinters in zones 8b–10.

Xanthosoma atrovirens 'Albomarginatum'

VARIEGATED ELEPHANT EAR

PRONOUNCED
zan-tho-SO-muh
at-ro-VY-renz

CARE NEEDS

EACH UNFURLING LEAF produced by *Xanthosoma* 'Albomarginatum' is a fresh delight, its blue-green surface edged with an irregular pattern of gray-green, soft sage, and creamy yellow. As the foliage expands to fifteen inches long, the cream portions change to bright white. The leaves curl at the tips, forming pouches that often prove watertight, making nifty cache-pockets for visiting insects to sip from. Where it's hardy, 'Albomarginatum' can reach five feet tall; used as an annual, three feet is more likely. Plant it in moist soil with bold *Musa basjoo*, delicate *Cyperus papyrus,* and the black-cherry blossoms of *Allamanda* 'Cherries Jubilee'. Overwinters in zones 9–10.

Xanthosoma 'Lime Zinger'

ALSO SOLD AS
'Chartreuse Giant',
'Golden Delicious',
X. maffafa 'Aurea'

PRONOUNCED
zan-tho-SO-muh

CARE NEEDS

AIRLINES ARE REPLACING their runway beacons and cities their streetlights with this fluorescent chartreuse elephant ear! Gorgeous color and jumbo size compel *Xanthosoma* 'Lime Zinger' to center stage in gardens, where its luminous eighteen-inch leaves borne on matching three- to six-foot stems make an eye-popping focal point. 'Lime Zinger' produces small plantlets snug against the mother bulb, forming a tight patch of sizzling color. Like other elephant ears, it grows best in moist soil. Purple *Thunbergia battescombei* and *Strobilanthes dyerianus* are cooling companions; or heat things up with *Ricinus* 'Carmencita', *Fuchsia* 'Gartenmeister Bonstedt', and *Oxalis* 'Aureus'. Overwinters in zones 9–10.

USDA WINTER HARDINESS ZONES

AVERAGE ANNUAL MINIMUM TEMPERATURE

Temperature (deg. C)			Zone	Temperature (deg. F)		
Below −45.5			1	Below −50		
−42.8	to	−45.5	2a	−45	to	−50
−40.0	to	−42.7	2b	−40	to	−45
−37.3	to	−40.0	3a	−35	to	−40
−34.5	to	−37.2	3b	−30	to	−35
−31.7	to	−34.4	4a	−25	to	−30
−28.9	to	−31.6	4b	−20	to	−25
−26.2	to	−28.8	5a	−15	to	−20
−23.4	to	−26.1	5b	−10	to	−15
−20.6	to	−23.3	6a	−5	to	−10
−17.8	to	−20.5	6b	0	to	−5
−15.0	to	−17.7	7a	5	to	0
−12.3	to	−15.0	7b	10	to	5
−9.5	to	−12.2	8a	15	to	10
−6.7	to	−9.4	8b	20	to	15
−3.9	to	−6.6	9a	25	to	20
−1.2	to	−3.8	9b	30	to	25
1.6	to	−1.1	10a	35	to	30
4.4	to	1.7	10b	40	to	35
Above 4.4			11	Above 40		